Also by Bill Watterson:

CALVIN AND HOBBES
SOMETHING UNDER THE BED IS DROOLING
YUKON HO!
WEIRDOS FROM ANOTHER PLANET
LAZY SUNDAY BOOK
REVENGE OF THE BABY-SAT
THE AUTHORITATIVE CALVIN AND HOBBES
SCIENTIFIC PROGRESS GOES 'BOINK'
ATTACK OF THE DERANGED MUTANT KILLER MONSTER SNOW GOONS
THE INDISPENSABLE CALVIN AND HOBBES
THE DAYS ARE JUST PACKED
HOMICIDAL PSYCHO JUNGLE CAT
THE ESSENTIAL CALVIN AND HOBBES
CALVIN AND HOBBES: THE TENTH ANNIVERSARY
THERE'S TREASURE EVERYWHERE
IT'S A MAGICAL WORLD

Taken from CALVIN AND HOBBES:
CALVIN AND HOBBES 1: THEREBY HANGS A TALE
CALVIN AND HOBBES 3: IN THE SHADOW OF THE NIGHT

Calvin and Hobbes

2: ONE DAY THE WIND WILL CHANGE

BILL WATTERSON

WARNER BOOKS

A *Warner* Book

First published in Great Britain in 1992
by Warner Books
Reprinted 1993, 1994, 1995, 1996, 1997

Copyright © 1987, 1992 by Bill Watterson,
distributed by Universal Press Syndicate
Calvin and Hobbes® is syndicated internationally by
Universal Press Syndicate

The contents of this edition were first published as part
of *Calvin and Hobbes* © 1987 by Bill Watterson, published by
Sphere Books 1988,
reprinted by Warner Books

ISBN 0 7515 0509 9

Printed in England by Clays Ltd, St Ives plc

Warner Books
A Division of
Little, Brown and Company (UK)
Brettenham House
Lancaster Place
London WC2E 7EN

A LITTLE LOWER ...OK, FINE!

THANKS FOR HELPING ME PUT UP THIS SWING.

WHERE DID YOU EVER FIND THIS GREAT TIRE?

CALVIN! I'VE GOT TO GO TO WORK!!

HEY, DOC, WHY ARE YOU RUBBING MY ARM WITH COTTON? ARE YOU GOING TO PUT A LEECH THERE?

ARE YOU GOING TO BLEED ME? YOU'RE NOT GOING TO AMPUTATE, ARE YOU? **ARE** YOU??

WHAT'S THAT? IS THAT A SHOT? ARE YOU GOING TO... **AAUGHH! IT WENT CLEAR THROUGH MY ARM!!** OW OW OW OW!!!

I'M DYING! I HOPE YOU'VE PAID YOUR MALPRACTICE INSURANCE, YOU QUACK!! **WHERE'S MY MOM??**

SOMEWHERE IN COMMUNIST RUSSIA I'LL BET THERE'S A LITTLE BOY WHO HAS NEVER KNOWN ANYTHING BUT **CENSORSHIP** AND **OPPRESSION**.

BUT MAYBE HE'S HEARD ABOUT **AMERICA**, AND HE DREAMS OF LIVING IN THIS LAND OF **FREEDOM** AND OPPORTUNITY!

SOMEDAY, I'D LIKE TO MEET THAT LITTLE BOY...

...AND TELL HIM THE AWFUL **TRUTH** ABOUT THIS PLACE!!

CALVIN, BE QUIET AND EAT THE STUPID LIMA BEANS.

MY SECRET ANCIENT TREASURE MAP SAYS TO DIG HERE!

LOOK! A WALLET FULL OF MONEY! RIGHT WHERE YOU SAID!

IT'S DAD'S. I BURIED IT HERE LAST WEEK.

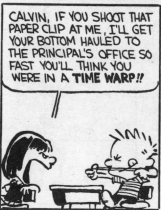

THE VALIANT SPACEMAN SPIFF IS BEING PURSUED BY A DISGUSTING SCUM BEING!

SPIFF SPOTS HIS HOVERING SPACESHIP AND BOLTS FOR THE LADDER!

BUT HE'S TOO LATE! THE AWFUL SCUM BEING IS UPON HIM! IT'S ALL OVER!

IT'S ALL OVER!!

I TOLD YOU **THREE TIMES** RECESS WAS OVER! NOW GET INSIDE!

You've got two periods to live, Twinky.

Then it's gym class, and I turn you into hamburger casserole!

I HATE GYM CLASS.

COACH THINKS VIOLENCE IS AEROBIC.

WATERSON

SPACEMAN SPIFF CLOSES IN ON THE ALIEN VESSEL!

THE ALIEN, BEING UNNATURALLY STUPID, IS BLISSFULLY IGNORANT OF ITS IMMINENT DOOM!

OUR HERO LOCKS ONTO TARGET AND WARMS UP HIS FRAP-RAY BLASTER!

MISS WORMWOOD!!

ZOUNDS! A GORKON DEATH STATION APPEARS! EVASIVE ACTION!

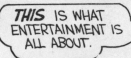

WE'VE GOT A BABY SITTER TONIGHT.

READY?

READY.

CALVIN, THE BABY SITTER IS HERE! WE'RE GOING! BE GOOD, OK?

LOST: MY TIGER, "HOBBES"

MAYBE YOU SHOULD DESCRIBE HIM.

ON THE QUIET SIDE. SOMEWHAT PECULIAR. A GOOD COMPANION, IN A WEIRD SORT OF WAY.

I MEAN, WHAT DOES HE LOOK LIKE?

OH.

WATERSON

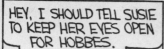

Other best selling Warner titles available by mail: